T0380812

benefits
OF THE CROSS

by **dr bo bryson**

A 30-DAY JOURNEY

WESTBOW
PRESS®
A DIVISION OF THOMAS NELSON
& ZONDERVAN

Editor: Grady W. Strop, Executive Director, RMI
(www.rejoiceministriesinternational.com)

Book design and layout: Sara Rankin

WestBow Press books may be ordered through booksellers or by contacting:

WestBow Press
A Division of Thomas Nelson & Zondervan
1663 Liberty Drive
Bloomington, IN 47403
www.westbowpress.com
844-714-3454

Other references: Brainy Quote (www.brainyquote.com), Mirriam-Webster
Online Dictionary (www.merriam-webster.com/dictionary) and specific
cited references noted within a devotional. The quotation on the back
cover is by Rev. Billy Graham (www.billygrahamlibrary.org)

ISBN: 979-8-3850-3368-3 (sc)
ISBN: 979-8-3850-3369-0 (e)

Library of Congress Control Number: 2024919835

Print information available on the last page.

WestBow Press rev. date: 09/20/2024

This devotional is dedicated to:
Those 'cloud of witnesses who help me run
with endurance the race set before me...'

(Hebrews 12:1-3)

TABLE OF BENEFITS

6   Endorsements

7   Foreword

9   Introduction

11   The Benefits

13   **access** | day 1

14   **child of God** | day 2

16   **confidence** | day 3

17   **deliverance** | day 4

18   **eternal life** | day 5

19   **forgiveness** | day 6

20   **freedom** | day 7

22   **friend of God** | day 8

23   **fruits of the spirit** | day 9

24   **gifts of the spirit** | day 10

25   **healing** | day 11

26   **heaven bound** | day 12

28   **holiness** | day 13

29   **inheritance** | day 14

30   **it is finished** | day 15

32   **death conquered** | day 16

33   **cleansing blood** | day 17

35   **joy in the morning** | day 18

36   **light to our eyes** | day 19

38   **love** | day 20

40   **no fear** | day 21

42   **power** | day 22

44   **redemption** | day 23

45   **renewed mind** | day 24

46   **restoration** | day 25

47   **the word** | day 26

48   **holy spirit** | day 27

50   **salvation** | day 28

52   **peace** | day 29

53   **passion** | day 30

55   Just the Beginning

56   Bonus Loop 1

58   Bonus Loop 2

59   Thought Life

60   About the Author

62   Notes

ENDORSEMENTS

"Dr. Bo takes readers on a journey to deeply ponder the redemptive work of the cross from many different angles as he explores Christ's potential impact on our lives. Through these quick daily introspective passages, we are challenged to consider the many opportunities and promises that God so lovingly wants to provide to each of us, if we will allow him. Starting each day with these faith-filled reminders is a nourishment for the soul."

Andrew Wilson, Training Manager – UBT

"Discover the transformative power of the cross in your daily life with this inspiring devotional! Through deep reflections and insights, Dr. Bo unveils how the cross offers healing, joy, power and so much more. Each day's reading draws you closer to understanding the profound love and sacrifice behind the cross, making this a must-read for anyone seeking to expand their appreciation for the greatest expression of love the world has ever known."

Sean Swihart, Lead Pastor – Crossroads Church

"Over the past twenty plus years I've had the privilege and blessing of knowing the author of what you are about to encounter in this brief, but impactful thirty-day devotional. I love Dr. Bo's practical approach and challenging nature to addressing the mysteries of Scripture and the power of the Cross! In the following pages you will be challenged to examine what you truly believe about the power of the cross and the discovery of resurrection life in Jesus Christ our Lord!"

Dick Dungan, Founder – Rejoice Ministries International

"I have known Dr. Bo for several years and loved his last book, Create a Trinity Lifestyle. This devotional is also very well written. I appreciate how it's not the typical daily devotional but instead, is spiritually challenging on multiple levels. I look forward to getting it into the hands of the people I work with. Great job Dr. Bo!"

Nate Kroll, Care Pastor – Christ Place church

"I like it. I appreciate that Dr. Bo focused on setting the reader up to engage with the cross through the daily readings and reflection questions. He is not necessarily telling the reader how to think but rather exposing them to what to think about and then leaving it between them and God. Well done!"

Kurt Earl, Associate A.D. and Bible teacher – LCS

FORWARD

The Cross. How often have you or I truly spent considerable time contemplating all the rich benefits the cross provides for us? Jesus' death on the cross did so much more than bring the possibility of the redemption of sin and victory over eternal death. The redemption it offers has the power to redeem so many concerns in our life which impact our lives right here, right now, in our daily lives.

Dr. Bo is offering to simply guide us on a journey of discovering these extra, substantial benefits the cross offers. He isn't defining what they are in detail as many devotional writers do. He is merely enticing us to go on the journey of examining and exploring the many wonders of the cross that we often have never perceived or considered for ourselves. Dr. Bo has encountered the abundance of life-giving reality of what Jesus brought through His sacrifice on the cross.

Now, he is inviting us to do the same.

I join him in inviting you to take this journey of contemplating 30 life-giving benefits Jesus offers us through His gift of yielding to the Father's plan for our full redemption. It's a significant opportunity to focus on the full legacy of the cross and its benefits for humankind. I believe everyone who takes this journey will find many personal gifts from the Father, Son and Holy Spirit.

May you receive all the Lord has for you!

Grady W Strop
President, Executive Director – Rejoice Ministries International

INTRODUCTION

When you think of the "benefits of the cross," what images or words come to mind? Let's even narrow down that statement, 'What comes to mind when you think of the cross?'

Pause ...

Pause again ...

Genuinely, what comes to mind? This is the starting place. How we view the cross speaks a great deal about how we view God and Christ, as well as our faith. The image that comes to my mind immediately is Jesus on the cross — bloody and bruised. But if I look deeper, what I see are His eyes. Eyes of purpose. Eyes of compassion. Eyes of expectation.

Hebrews 12:2 says it this way: "...looking to Jesus, the founder and perfecter of our faith, who for the joy that was set before him endured the cross, despising its shame, and is seated at the right hand of the throne of God."

AW Tozer is quoted as saying, "What comes into our minds when we think about God is the most important thing about us." The most important thing! The cross causes us to look at Jesus. Jesus, the One who was from the beginning and is at the end. The One who through all things are made. The One who makes all things new. The One, hanging in anguish and pain on the cross. This Jesus, with eyes of purpose, compassion and expectation—looked not only at the cross but through the cross and saw so much more than what those around Him saw. Others saw torture. Jesus saw redemption. Others saw shame. Jesus saw hope. Others saw the end. Jesus saw the beginning. Others saw the enemy. Jesus saw the Father. Jesus saw you. And seeing you and the love of His Father for each of us, He was able to "for the joy that was set before Him endure the cross."

Jesus endured. For you. For me.

The benefits of the cross. Pause...

(

"Bless the Lord, O my soul, and
FORGET NOT ALL HIS BENEFITS,
who forgives all your iniquity, who heals all your diseases,
who redeems your life from the pit,
who crowns you with steadfast love and mercy,
who satisfies you with good so that your youth
is renewed like the eagle's."

Psalm 103:2-5

THE BENEFITS

Benefit is defined as:

(1) Noun: something that produces good or helpful results or effects or that promotes well-being.

(2) Verb: to be useful or profitable

Why does that matter?

The benefit presented each day is simply a noun. It is the good and helpful result of the cross. Your journey is to read and meditate on how that benefit moves from being a noun to becoming a verb. Meaning: How does that benefit not only help your own life but also become profitable and useful in the lives of others?

The question you may have right now is, why? Why should I pursue turning the noun into a verb? Think of it this way. You are the soil. The benefit you will read each day is a seed full of potential for growth (i.e. a noun). As you read, the seed will be 'planted in you.' This seed, if it is to grow, must be nourished and cared for (i.e. the benefit must be meditated on and put into practice). The caring of the seed is the process of turning the noun into a verb. It really is that simple but it will take work. Do not let the seed stay dormant. Let it grow into something spectacular. Philippians 2:12-13 says it this way, "...work out your own salvation with fear and trembling, for it is God who works in you, both to will and to work for his good pleasure." You can also read Mark 6:30-32 to see how a seed (noun) becomes useful for others (verb).

If you are ready to grow that seed, to turn that noun into a verb, to work out your salvation — then turn the page. But, before you do.

Pause ...

... and remember this, Jesus may have died on the cross, but He is not dead. He conquered the grave. He is alive and active in our lives. HE IS ACTIVE IN OUR LIVES! And that, my friends, is the most amazing benefit of all.

Two other thoughts:

(1.) Each benefit, although 'big' in importance, is meant to be small in writing. I kept it short for a reason. I wanted you to be able to think vertically but then respond horizontally. What do I mean by that? Simply this: what you think about affects how you live with yourself and with others. May you think about the benefits of the cross and respond appropriately. Some verses are written out. Others are not, so you would have to look them up. After each benefit, there are reflection questions with a space to write your own thoughts.

(2.) 1 Corinthians 1:18 reads, "For the message of the cross is foolishness to those who are perishing, but to us who are being saved it is the power of God." As you read, if these benefits do not make sense/seem foolish to you, stop and ask yourself this question: Do I just like the teachings of Jesus or have I committed my life to follow Him? There is a difference and the cross unlocks the power of that difference. And that difference will make the benefits come alive if your life!

Note: For all devotions, remember to look up the scripture references found within each devotional. It will make your time more meaning-FULL.

access

Before the cross, only the high priest had access to the Holy inner room in the "Tabernacle of Moses". And that was only once per year. Once per year! (Read Hebrews 9:6-14 for reference.) Can you imagine only being able to communicate with God once a year? What would you say? What would be going through your mind as you crossed the threshold of the Tabernacle?

day 1

But the cross provided an indescribable benefit. I mean, come on! Can you imagine it? The veil was torn, top to bottom! It was like God was tearing all that hindered our access to Him. (Matthew 27:51, Mark 15:38, Luke 23:45). No one comes to the Father except through Christ (John 14:6). The cross gave us access to the Father! Access to the Holy of Holies! We can come to him crying, Abba, Father! We can come boldly before Him, knowing He is a good Father. Think about it; the God of the universe allows me access to Himself. Wow, what a benefit!

~~~~~~~~~~~~~~~~~~~~~~~~~~~~

REFLECTION

Consider for a moment the implications of the veil being torn from top to bottom. How does this impact your access to God?

child of God

If you are a parent, you know your child needs two things: love and discipline (aka: training). As a child of God, we are no different. Love sets us free to experience and grow. Discipline keeps us safe in the midst of this growth. I think of a verse, Hebrews 12:6,11, "For the Lord disciplines the one he loves ... For the moment all discipline seems painful rather than pleasant, but later it yields the peaceful fruit of righteousness to those who have been trained by it."

God loves us and because of the cross, He gives us the right to become children (John 1:25, Romans 8:16). Think about it; we are no longer orphans wandering around wondering whose or who we are. In the midst of our wandering, discipline may come but as seen above, it produces righteousness. This 'training' gives us (the children) three very powerful "I's" we can use to defeat the lies of the enemy:

(1) Identity: Two of the most important questions you can ever answer are. Who is God? Who am I? Knowing you are His child is a game-changer for how you relate to yourself and others.

(2) Involvement: We get to participate with God in bringing His purpose to earth. He does not need to do this but He chooses to involve His children.

(3) Inheritance: As a child, all He has is ours. All He has is yours. Mind-blowing!

~~~~~~

REFLECTION

Do you believe you are a child of God?

Identity: Is He a good Father? Who are you in Him?

Involvement: How have you participated with God? Is there
something you would like to participate in with Him?

Inheritance: More on this later but for now, look up these verses:
1 Peter 1:3-4; Ephesians 1:11-14 and Colossians 3:23-24. How does
your inheritance in Jesus impact the way you live your life?

confidence

Confidence is defined as: the belief that one can rely on someone or something; firm trust.

To whom or what do you place your firm and full trust? Yourself? A job? A family member or friend? Those are not wrong inherently but anything other than God will disappoint eventually. It is inevitable.

God will not disappoint. You may not feel confident at times; that is normal. But stay "steadfast, immovable, always abounding in the work of the Lord, knowing that in the Lord your labor is not in vain." (1 Corinthians 15:58). The cross is God's plan and purpose for mankind. Your confidence can come from the fact that the cross bears witness to His love (a benefit to be discussed later). But for now, know this: in that love, we can have a confident hope and a future regardless of our present circumstances.

Can you put your full faith and trust in the One who offers a confidence not dependent upon anyone or anything in this world's circumstances, troubles, or trials?

~~~~~~~~~~~~~~~~~~~~~~~~~~~~~~~~

REFLECTION

What does the word confidence bring to your mind?

How can confidence in Jesus' sacrifice on the cross help you face the daily challenges of life?

deliverance

Jesus' death on the cross delivered us. But, delivered us from what? Galatians 1:4 reminds us that Jesus " ... who gave himself for our sins to deliver us from the present evil age, according to the will of our God and Father." Yes, we are delivered from the shackles of sin. Death was and is defeated by His death and resurrection. But my question is this: if we are delivered and sin is defeated, why do many of us live defeated lives? Could it be that we do not believe the cross delivers us from sin? Or could it be that we don't realize in delivering us from sin; He also came to give life and life to the fullest; not just for eternity, but for now — today! (John 10:10).

day 4

Besides our sins; we are also delivered from the law and the weight of guilt/shame. (see Romans 8:1 and Galatians 3:13) We are delivered from our past and the lies that bombard us about not only our identity but His. Remember, our sins are as far as the east is from the west (Psalm 103:12). As we look at the cross and seek the Lord, let us not forget, He not only answers us but delivers us from our fears and becomes our hiding place (Psalm 34:4, Psalm 32:7-8).

REFLECTION

How do you think Jesus' death on the cross can help you gain deliverance from your shame, past hurts, etc?

What is it to be free from sin? Or, from the law?

eternal life

day 5

One of the best known verses points to the cross and its impact on eternal life. John 3:16 reads, "For God so loved the world, that he gave his only Son, that whoever believes in him should not perish but have eternal life." What is eternal life? It is best defined by the words of John 17:3: "And this is eternal life, that they know you, the only true God, and Jesus Christ whom you have sent." Jesus himself says it plainly, "Truly, truly, I say to you, whoever hears my word and believes him who sent me has eternal life..." To look at the cross ... to gaze at Jesus...to believe...that is eternal life.

Furthermore, Ecclesiastes 3:11 reminds us; "...he has put eternity into man's heart.." I wonder how often I think in terms of eternity. Meaning this, life — the physicality of it — is but a vapor (James 4:14). Where is my thought process on the daily? What do I think about most often? As I look at those around me, do I think or consider the importance of where others will spend eternity? You see, my (our) view of eternal life will most definitely shape our view of heaven, hell and God. John 11:25 & John 17:2 speak of Jesus being the resurrection and the life. Eternal life is found in the person of Jesus; period!

REFLECTION

What do you believe about the Cross and its connection to eternal life?

If life is but a vapor, how are you spending your time?

forgiveness

Those who are forgiven much, love much. (Luke 7:47) Do you realize you have been forgiven much?

I think of my wife's forgiveness. She showed me practically the love of Christ through her forgiveness. That changed my view of the cross forever. It was a gift I did not deserve. We must see forgiveness as a gift (Roman 5:15). We can do nothing to earn it nor do we deserve it. I believe the reality of unconditional forgiveness messes with us because we are wired to want to do something to earn it.

day 6

I heard someone say the other day, "I will forgive them when they do (fill in the blank)." That is not forgiveness. It is manipulation and control. If we are to receive forgiveness, we must first realize that we need it and then we must recognize we can do nothing to earn it. Can we do that? At first glance, I think we can, but when we dig a little deeper, we often find we've put strategies in place in our lives to earn, to keep up, to prove the forgiveness is not wasted, etc. Isn't that like saying, the forgiveness of the cross was not good enough because now I must add my 'good works' to make it complete. Really?

Two other verses to consider.

(1) Romans 4:7, "Blessed are those whose lawless deeds are forgiven, and whose sins are covered..."

(2) 1 John 4:19, "We love because he first loved us."

~~~~~~~~~~~~~~~~~~~~~~~~~~~

REFLECTION

How does Jesus' death on the Cross teach you about how you should forgive?

Have you had to forgive someone? If so, how did it change you?

Based on the forgiveness shown to you, how has that changed your love for people around you?

freedom

I sent a text to a friend that read, "UR loved and UR free. Believe it and walk in it!"

We are simply free — true and complete. Yet, why do we live all bound up and chained? Do we really like prison that much? It would seem so at times. As discussed in the 'Deliverance devo' we are set free from sin, guilt and shame. But even more, we are set free from the lie that we can be in control; our own God. (See Genesis 3:1-7)

Three verses to ponder:

(1) Galatians 5:1, "For freedom Christ has set us free; stand firm therefore, and do not submit again to a yoke of slavery." Why did God set us free? It is so we would not submit again to slavery; a way of thinking and living that says we have to 'work for His love and approval.'

(2) 2 Corinthians 3:17, "Where the spirit of the Lord is, there is freedom." If we believe He sent the Holy Spirit to dwell with/ within us; then we have freedom!

(3) 1 Peter 2:16-17, "Live as people who are free, not using your freedom as a cover-up for evil, but living as servants of God." Honor everyone. Love the brotherhood. Fear God. Honor the emperor. Our freedom in Christ should give us reason to love and honor others all the more.

Freedom comes with great responsibility. Being a slave in many ways is easier. At times, I think we would rather have it easier. You know, go back to Egypt even if in bondage (at least we know what to do and not to do) vs being free and responsible for taking the promised land before us. Why? Because freedom requires faith, work and courage. Freedom comes with a price but not a price we pay. The price has been paid on the cross. Let's not take our freedom for granted.

REFLECTION

Which of the previous verses stood out to you and why?

Do you feel free in Christ? If not, why?

How can I learn to live/walk in the freedom Christ offers through His complete redemptive work on the cross?

friend of God

What? God and I are friends. Absurd, 100%. Truth, 100%.

I think about my own relationship with my dad. Not that I ever was a slave or servant, but I had to learn obedience and "how to act" and what to do and not do. Furthermore, I learned that I was his son, a beloved child, an heir to all that is his. Now, although I am still his son; a transition has occurred. I am older and we have become friends. It is a rich, mutually beneficial relationship because I not only realize who I am but who he is. This earthly reality took me a while to believe but it is true.

And, because of the cross, I believe the same can be said of our relationship with God. Many, if not most, come to a relationship with Christ with a servant mentality (how do I act, what can I do or not do, etc.). We serve and serve but yet somehow still feel unfulfilled. At some point, God reveals our own heart and His heart to us about our son/daughtership and it is like an explosion inside our being. We are blown away that we can call him "Abba" but then a transition occurs. We become friends! As James 2:23 says, "... and he was called the friend of God." Servant ... Beloved child ... Friend — we are all these. (John 15:15 and Galatians 4:7)

You see, I want to serve not necessarily out of duty but because I am loved. I also want to bless and encourage my friend. To be a friend of God—does it get any sweeter?

~~~~~~~~~~~~~~

REFLECTION

Would you describe God as a friend? If not, why?

You are a friend of God. That is the truth! But, if God had to describe your friend's status on social media, what 3 words would he use?

Read Psalm 25:14. *Do you serve God out of obligation and duty, as a servant? Or, do you serve and obey God out of thanksgiving and gratefulness?*

fruits of the spirit

The cross was supposed to produce death. However, it produced fruit that gives life and life abundantly. What fruit? Love, joy, peace, patience, kindness, goodness, faithfulness, gentleness and self-control. (Galatians 5:22-23). I guess the question I must ask myself: Am I bearing this fruit?

day 9

I think of a quote by Henri Nouwen, "Did I offer peace today? Did I bring a smile to someone's face? Did I say words of healing? Did I let go of my anger and resentment? Did I forgive? Did I love? These are the real questions. I must trust that the little bit of love that I sow now will bear many fruits, here in this world and the life to come."

~~~~~~~~~~~~~~~~~~~~~~~~~~~

REFLECTION

What 'fruit' found in the verse above do you most easily relate to?

Which 'fruit' found in the above verse do you most struggle with?

gifts of the spirit

A question that pops into my head is, do the gifts come before the fruit or the other way around or does it matter? Fruits and gifts — how and why are they different? I am unsure if I have the answer to that one but I came across a blog post which describes it well. (http://spiritofthelordgod.blogspot.com/2011/11/gifts-fruit-of-spirit.html)

This blog post goes into detail about the gifts. I like the way the author separates them into 3 categories. "They can be divided into three types, which include: the speaking gifts (tongues, interpretation of tongues, and prophecy), the knowing gifts (word of knowledge, word of wisdom, and discerning of spirits) and the power gifts (faith, healing, miracles)." The author even does a side-by-side comparison of the gifts!

Does the cross not point to a gift also? The gift of salvation. Ephesians 2:8-9 reads, "For by grace you have been saved through faith. And this is not your own doing; it is the gift of God [on the cross], not a result of works, so that no one may boast." (Emphasis added). Then, I thought, what is the purpose of a gift? In general, it is to bless or encourage someone else, correct? Did not salvation do that for us? Are the gifts of the Spirit any different? God gives gifts for the common good of all people and not all people have the same gifting. (1 Corinthians 12: 7, 1 Corinthians 12: 27). The question for us: do we use the gifts of the Spirit to help the fruits of the Spirit grow and mature? Or, do we take the gifts for granted causing the fruit to be choked out and die (see last devo for discussion on fruits of the Spirit)?

Bottom line, God has given each of us a gift. Use them to bless and encourage. But a word of caution. "Don't compare; it is the thief of joy." T. Roosevelt said this many years ago and it is still true today.

~~~~~~~~~~~~~~~~~~~~~

REFLECTION

You have a gift (we all do). Do you know what yours is?

How are you using your gift to bless, encourage and build up others?

healing

Two verses come to mind: (1) 1 Peter 2:24, "He himself bore our sins in his body on the tree, that we might die to sin and live to righteousness. By his wounds you have been healed." (2) Isaiah 53:5, "But he was pierced for our transgressions; he was crushed for our iniquities; upon him was the chastisement that brought us peace, and with his wounds we are healed." Jesus on the cross: pierced, crushed, wounded. Those wounds — His wounds — healed then and still heals today.

day 11

The next logical question to ask is, healed from what? Physical sickness? Mental pain? Heartache? Death? Sin? Then a follow up verse comes to mind, "I have said these things to you, that in me you may have peace. In the world you will have tribulation [trouble]. But take heart; I have overcome the world." (John 16:33d). Clearly then, He has not healed us from heartache since we will experience trouble (it is not a 'may have' but rather a 'will have').

Ok, now what? I remember praying for my brother-in-law to be healed from cancer. He was not. How do I (we) respond to that? I think if we are not careful, we can look at healing (mainly physical) or more specifically lack thereof and become disappointed in God for not "coming through." We then think; God must not care and thus is not good. What a lie; however, we still have to work through feelings of loss, hurt and frustration. And that is ok. God gives grace for that.

Furthermore, physical healing is often all we consider — probably because it is what we see with our natural eyes. My brother-in-law was not healed physically but he was healed in so many other ways during his cancer. I personally think the biggest thing His wounds heal is the lie that we are not loved or valued by God himself. Heal that lie and the world changes!

REFLECTION

Have you blamed God for not healing you or a loved one?

What hurt do you need to bring to God for healing?

heaven bound

Philippians 3:20 reads, 'But our citizenship is in heaven ... "

day 12

Have you ever considered what the actual word 'christian' means? 'Christ' refers to Jesus Christ. Regardless if someone believes in him or not, history and evidence proves he was real. He was beaten, put on a cross, and was not found in the grave. Furthermore, 'ian' means, "belonging to or having characteristics of.' Thus, the meaning of being a Christian is someone who belongs to Christ or has characteristics of Christ. Did not Jesus tell the disciples to have 'His character?' He said in Matthew 16:24, "If anyone would come after me, let him deny himself and take up his cross and follow me." Something to think about next time we call ourselves christian. Why is this important? Because I think it points to not only how we affect the here and now but where our citizenship (eternal home) is.

I think some people only "get-saved" so they can go to heaven. Or is it because they do not want to go to hell? That is a problem because although our citizenship is in heaven, let us not forget we are still on planet earth. We need to set our mind on things above (eternity minded) so we can affect the here and now (earthly reality). Didn't Christ do the same? He set his mind on things above (His father's business) so he could affect the earthly reality (people's lives) around him. (See John 5:19-20)

Last thought: if I am heaven bound, am I trying to take others with me or am I content going on my own journey? If I am honest, it is both and depends on the day. But I want to keep it in front of me. Ecclesiastes 3:11 (NLT) states, "God has made everything beautiful for its own time. He has planted eternity in the human heart, but even so, people cannot see the whole scope of God's work from beginning to end." Eternity is planted in every human heart; it just needs to be called forth. Let's call it forth!

REFLECTION

How does the definition of being a Christian affect your daily life?

How should being eternity minded affect your daily life?

holiness

What comes to mind when you read the word holiness? Sterile, upright, not fun? The first thing that comes to my mind is a quote I read by DL Moody. He writes regarding the Bible, "This book will keep you from sin or sin will keep you from this book." We often swing from generation to generation depending on the cultural influence of our time. Could it be time for some holiness to be introduced back into our culture? But not a holiness that creates guilt and shame but rather a holiness that creates life and freedom in Christ (remember, he came to give us life abundantly). The question is, how to do it? How do we walk in freedom and holiness at the same time? Maybe it is looking at the cross and recognizing Christ embodied both. He was a Holy sacrifice that washed away our sins giving us freedom to love and be loved. (See Hebrews 10:1-20.)

We have both! But a thought comes to my mind: are we scared of both? If I am holy, can I really be free? If I am free, will I mess up holiness? Ahhhhhhhhhhh ... what are we to do? We are to be conformed to the image of God (Romans 8:29). How? By living out 1 Peter 1:13-25, a call to be holy.

REFLECTION

Do you lean more toward holiness or freedom as you think about your faith?

What part of 1 Peter 1:13-25 stands out to you most?

inheritance

In order to think about having an inheritance, you need to be someone's child. By the cross, we are grafted into God's family ('a chosen people, a royal priesthood' 1 Peter 2:9). We are entitled to the inheritance not by anything we have done but by all His doing. He chose to bring heaven to earth instead of us trying to climb our way to heaven.

day 14

The definition of inheritance is: 'something or someone's property that can be inherited.' What is the 'something or someone's property' that we have inherited? Is it not Christ Himself in the form of the Holy Spirit (John 16:7). I wonder how many times I think the inheritance is another gift (material blessing, etc.). instead of realizing Christ himself is the gift. Then I am reminded of Matthew 6:33, "But seek first the kingdom of God and his righteousness, and all these things will be added to you."

Two other verses:

(1) Psalm 16:5-11, "The Lord is my portion. My inheritance!" As I set that idea before me, pleasures are found. Pleasures!

(2) Lamentations 3:24, "The Lord is my inheritance, so I put my hope in Him." Anything other than the Lord being our whole inheritance will surely disappoint. Let's not be disappointed — let us know where our pleasure lies!

REFLECTION

What part of Psalm 16:5-11 speaks most to you?

What does 'seek first His kingdom' look like in your daily life?

it is finished

The first question that pops into my head is: Really? Are you sure I don't need to add to the cross? My extra effort? My strengths? My grit? My 'whatever' does not add too, or enhance the finished work. The second question that arises into my head is: do I believe it is finished? Do my actions speak to that truth?

day 15

John Piper says it this way: "One of the greatest things Jesus ever said was, "It is finished" (John 19:30). Jesus was saying, My obedience is finished and perfect, and you need it. My suffering is finished, and you need it to cover all your sins. I have finished removing the wrath of God from my people. I have finished striking Satan with a death blow. I have established a new covenant for my people. It is finished. And, because it is finished, the mission begins."

The mission begins! This thought goes far behind this devotional but the mission can be summed up like this: Our mission is to understand the finished work of the cross and how that should impact our daily living!

I also read this. "What Jesus did through His perfect earthly existence, sacrificial death, and glorious resurrection fully completed the work the Father had given Him to do. Not only did He complete His salvific work, but His accomplishment is fully efficacious, today and will be forevermore. There is nothing more to add — nothing more to be done by God, man, or religious institutions. The undeniable, factual, historic, and eternal work of Jesus Christ has been completed—is complete—and will forever remain completed. "IT ... IS ... FINISHED!" You can read the whole article: https://carm.org/devotion-it-is-finished.

~~~~~~~~~~~~~~~~~~~~~~~~~~~~~~~~~~~~

REFLECTION

*How does the finished work of the cross affect your daily life?
Have you thought about it before?*

*How has that now, or in the future, been or become a practical
reality?*

death conquered

Jesus may have finished the work on the cross but the fact that He was raised back to life is literally life-giving. It gives us hope, joy, and the incredible promise of John 10:10 (that he came to give life and life to the fullest). Without the resurrection, there is no life — only death.

A question to consider: Do I walk in the reality of the warning and promise of John 10:10? Do I realize the threat of the enemy but at the same time the gift of a full life? How does that affect my mindset as I approach each day?

John Piper writes, "No death for us, no resurrection for us, no presence at God's right hand for us, no intercession for us would do us any good if it were not Jesus Christ who died and rose and reigns and intercedes. So let's keep our focus on him. Look to him. Know him. We are not talking about a mythological event or a random deed or a mere human happening. We are seeing the historical Jesus Christ in action. And the point is to know HIM as our security."

You can read the entire blog post if you choose: https://www.desiringgod.org/messages/the-all-conquering-love-of-christ

REFLECTION

Thinking about the above Piper quote...Where is your focus?

Read John 10:10. What is the threat? What is the promise? How does knowing those affect your day to day thinking?

cleansing blood

For this benefit, we will look at a few verses:

day 17

(1) Acts 20:28, "... which he obtained by His very own blood." What did he obtain? The church, which is you and I. He obtained his treasured possession! What did it cost him — everything! What did it cost us — nothing! A radical exchange that we do not fully grasp.

(2) Revelations 1:5, "To him who loves us and has freed us from our sins by His blood." His love led Him to bleed and that blood led us to be cleansed.

(3) Isaiah 53:5, "By his stripes we are healed ..." His stripes are blood-laden and we are healed because of that.

(4) Isaiah 1:18, " ... we are washed whiter than snow ..." I look out at a fresh snow and see the beauty of it and then think of this verse. We are washed that white — that clean — that beautiful ... then as if nature tells the story, the snow darkens from dirt, grime and it looks no longer white but gray and then black. The world taints beauty. The world layers the shades of gray to make us believe the cleansing never happened. Let us walk with faith to know we are cleansed!

(5) Revelation 12:11, 'They overcome by the blood of the lamb and the word of their testimony, for they loved not their lives even unto death." This is one of my favorite texts in the bible. How do we overcome? Two things: His blood and our testimony about what that blood changed and gives to our life. We cannot add to His blood and our testimony cannot be taken away.

The question that comes to my mind: Do I believe in His blood and is my testimony a one-time experience or an on-going, intentional and deepening (even if at times slow) relationship with Him? Because if my testimony is 50% of what overcomes, then should I not be concerned with how it is being written and/or spoken out; not only here on earth but in the heavenlies.

(6) 1 Peter 1:18-19, " ... knowing that you were ransomed [bought/ paid for in full] from the futile ways inherited from your forefathers, not with perishable things such as silver or gold, but with the precious blood of Christ, like that of a lamb without blemish or spot ..." Anything other than His blood will not satisfy. Everything else is perishable. Anything other than His blood, even if costly, would not ransom you or I.

~~~~~~~~~~~~~~~~~~~~~~~~

REFLECTION

Do you live as if we know the price that was paid? If so, would it/should it not change the way we interact with the Father and others? What would that look like in my daily life? How might my life need to change?

joy in the morning

Three verses to consider with this benefit:

(1) Psalm 30:5, " ... weeping may last for a night but joy comes in the morning." Whether it is literally one night, or a season of life, or a specific event; weeping will not last! There is joy and that joy is real and is found only in the crucified and risen Christ.

(2) Nehemiah 8:10, " ... do not grieve for the joy of the Lord is my strength." His joy = my strength. More on this below.

(3) Hebrews 12:2, "...fixing our eyes on Jesus, the author and perfecter of our faith. For the joy set before him he endured the cross, scorning its shame ..." For joy ... He endured shame, humiliation, being beat and spat upon; even death. He did all that ... for the joy?? Not sure I would associate joy with the cross but He did.

His joy = my strength? What type of joy? The same joy that Christ went to cross with, a joy that is deep, rich and vibrant. A joy that no matter the circumstances and how long they last ("the night"), it is that joy that comes in the morning. It is what you feel and know when you sing, "Joy to the World," because only that joy changes hearts. It is only that joy that causes us to be in wonderment of His love. Joy in the morning? Yes, it's really available but we must fix our eyes on the one in whom joy is found. Where are your eyes fixed?

REFLECTION

Where are you looking for joy? How do you distinguish between happiness and joy?

You were the 'joy set before Him' when He endured the cross. Have you ever considered that He enjoys you?

light to our eyes

"I am the light of the world ... let us fix our eyes on Jesus ..."
(John 8:12 & Hebrews 12:2).

The same question that I asked on day 18, 'Joy in the Morning', comes into play here as well (and maybe all of them actually): Where are your eyes fixed? On the light or do we keep our eyes closed so we can not see the light? We say we do not like the darkness but is that really true? My father-in-law said to me once that nothing good happens after 10 p.m. It made me laugh because it is partially true. When do most "bad things" happen — in the dark, hidden! That makes me wonder, are we hiding like Adam and Eve, in the shade of the bushes (darkness)? Like them, we don't believe we deserve to be seen or we don't want to yield to His promise of Love. The lie of the enemy has taken hold in our lives, "we can be our own God." However, God wants to free us from the lie and bring us into the light so we can be saved, redeemed, restored, free!

A few more verses:

(1) John 3:19, "And this is the judgment: the light has come into the world, and people loved the darkness rather than the light ..." Judgment, that is a strong word. We see the light but choose the darkness. And, here is the kicker, when I think of choosing darkness, I think of sneaking around in the dark — murder, breaking in, etc ... but is not the darkness also found in gossip, envy, pride, etc.. and although those are displayed in the light, they sure are in the dark. Let us love the light more than the darkness!

(2) John 1:5, "The light shines in the darkness and the darkness has not overcome it." (John 1:5) What a promise! His light in us can overcome. All we must do is let it shine. Cue kid's song, "This little light of mine, I'm gonna let it shine ..."

(3) Matthew 5:16, "In the same way, let your light shine before others, so that they may see your good works and give glory to your Father who is in heaven". The light we show is to be that of Christ not our own. But how often do I let my "own light" shine?

(4) 1 John 1:5-7 "This is the message we have heard from him and proclaim to you, that God is light, and in him is no darkness at all. If we say we have fellowship with him while we walk in darkness, we lie and do not practice the truth. But if we walk in the light, as he is in the light, we have fellowship with one another, and the blood of Jesus his Son cleanses us from all sin." The blood and our proclamation of truth (testimony) as discussed earlier, are both game changers!

The old adage holds true here: 'Don't just talk the talk … walk the walk.' If we say we walk in the light, let's make sure our actions follow.

~~~~~~~~~~~~~~~~~~

REFLECTION

How do you let His light shine through you?

Again, I will ask: where are your eyes fixed?

love

Love. What is love? Which kingdom do we get our definition from? God's definition of love or the worlds'? For myself, if I'm not careful, I mix the two to make some sort of "love potion." From the outside, this potion may look more appealing but it is a weaker, watered down version of the real thing. And who wants that? I would rather have a love tonic: pure, simple and strong! That is God's love.

We often say, "Yeah, I know God loves me but ..." But what? There is no but! None! He loves me. Period. Anything else following that statement is false. It is a lie or our own issues, not His. We layer issues and excuses to discount His incredible love. What did that love cost him? Everything. And how often do we neglect it, overlook it, discount it or worse yet, not receive it on a daily basis when He offers it freely. It really is mind-blowing if you stop and think about the exchange. He gets beaten; we get love. He gets nailed to a cross; we get love. He gets killed; we get love.

A few verses:

(1) 1 John 4:10, "And this is love, not that we have loved God but that he loved us and sent his Son to be the propitiation for our sins" What is love? The verse lays out the definition. Why do we try to add to it?

(2) 1 John 3:16, "By this we know love, that he laid down his life for us, and we ought to lay down our lives for our brothers." How do we know? Look at the cross!

(3) John 13:35, "By this you will be known ... if you love one another ..." We are known by the way we love? With that perspective, we may want to consider how we are loving others.

(4) 1 Cor. 13, "The love chapter." People can quote it, even read it at their wedding, but quoting it is not the same as living it. What I find interesting is the end of the verse, " ... you can have all but if you have not love, you have nothing!" Nothing, really? That seems extreme. But if we stop and think about it, it is quite true. Without love, we have nothing of worth. We might have lots of material stuff, even religious and spiritual good works, but, in the end, we have nothing.

(5) Phil. 1:9-11, "And it is my prayer that your love may abound more and more, with knowledge and all discernment, so that you may approve what is excellent, and so be pure and blameless for the day of Christ, filled with the fruit of righteousness that comes through Jesus Christ, to the glory and praise of God." Love that would abound. Love that is wise. Love that is discerning. Love that brings glory and praise. That's the love I want!

"... by this we know love ... by love you will be known." However, let us not forget the most significant piece of love; it has a name: Jesus! He offered this love through the Cross!

~~~~~~~~~~~~~~~~~~~~~~~

REFLECTION

How is His love different from any other love in the world?

How are you known — Your love? Your achievements?
Your social posts?

no fear

The first question that comes to my mind is this: Is it even possible to live with no fear? We live in a fallen world where there is danger all around. Are we not to fear things that could hurt our children, ourselves, etc. I think we are supposed to be cautious at times—wise and discerning—but is that different than fear? I think so. I think fear has to do with control. It has to do with where my gaze is set: on the fearful circumstance or the God who casts out all fear. And I think it is ok to be initially fearful but then turn our gaze toward God to let fear subside. As people say, "let Go and let God." But wow...that's hard at times.

A few verses:

(1) Psalms 23:4 (NLT), "Even when I walk through the darkest valley, I will not be afraid, for you are close beside me ..." We do not have to fully understand but we need to fully recognize his presence because that recognition changes our perspective.

(2) Isaiah 43:1, "Fear not, for I have redeemed you, I have called you by name, you are mine." Look close; it is not in my own power that I am redeemed. It is by His power. It is because He calls me His own and because I am His, I do not have to fear. A great benefit of the Cross!

(3) Joshua 1:9, " ... do not be discouraged and do not be afraid for the Lord the God is with you wherever you go." A declaration and promise we see over and over in the Old Testament but still applies to our life today!

Below is a summary based on Isaiah 41:10. It is titled, the "Five Pillars of Fearlessness". It is written by John Piper. You can read the entire post here: https://www.desiringgod.org/messages/fear-not-i-am-with-you-i-am-your-god.

It was too good not to share a small portion.

1. I am your God — **over you.**

2. I am with you — **by your side.**

3. I will strengthen you — **from inside of you.**

4. I will help you — **all around you from wherever the enemy comes.**

5. I will uphold you — **from underneath you.**

Let me summarize in my own words. Over you, by you, inside you, around you, underneath you. Therefore, do not fear! That is powerful.

~~~~~~~~~~~~~~~~~~~~~~~~~~~~

REFLECTION

What causes you the most fear? Why?

If there is no "fear in the love of God" how should that change the way I live?

power

1 Corinthians 1:18 reads, "For the word of the cross is folly to those who are perishing, but to us who are being saved it is the power of God."

day 22

The power of God. Hmmmm?

What is power? Webster defines it as: "the ability to perform in a certain way with quality or the ability to influence others or events." With that being the definition; do we not have all the potential of being powerful? We all can perform with quality if we choose, and we all can and do have influence. The question is: where does our power come from? God or self-reliance, knowledge, experience, or the need for approval/advancement? Since we all have access to power, I think we may want to check our motives.

Marcus Aurelius said, "You have power over your mind — not outside events. Realize this, and you will find strength." Did you catch that? We can have power over ourselves not others or outside circumstances. I think of another quote by Jon Wooden that states, "Discipline yourself so others do not have to." Woah!

Another verse comes to mind, "... for God gave us a spirit not of fear but of power and love and self-control." (2 Tim. 1:7) We are given power and that power does not come from ourselves but rather from the very spirit of God! It is the power of the cross working in and through us.

Two verses:

(1) Exodus 9:16, "I have raised you up for a purpose ... that I might show my power and my name throughout the earth." How many times do we (I) ask, 'what is my purpose?' Well, could it be this verse playing itself out in our lives; for him to show His power and His name through us?

(2) Acts 1:8, "You will receive power when the Holy Spirit comes upon you and you will be my witnesses ..." Why do we receive the Holy Spirit? Power, but power to do what? Witness, but witness to do what? Witnesses of the power of the cross and His name throughout the earth.

~~~~~~~~~~~~~~~~~~~~~

REFLECTION

Do you feel like you are powerful? If not, why not?

Are you using the power God gave you to witness His name throughout the earth (your area of influence)? If not, why not?

redemption

Webster defines redemption as: "the act or process of redeeming."
Redeeming is defined as: "serving to offset or compensate for a
defect."

So this definition begs the question: What defect needs offsetting
or compensated for in regard to ...? Is it not the lie from the
beginning of time that we can "be like God"? This lie caused
a massive defect in the fabric of humanity; separation from
the Father. And the only way to rectify this defect is Christ's
compensation, His redeeming love, His love demonstrated on the
cross. This is the redemption we need.

A few verses:

(1) Romans 3:23-24, " ... all have sinned and fall short of the glory
of God, being justified as a gift by His grace through the
redemption which is in Christ Jesus ..." All have sinned, thus,
all need redemption.

(2) Ephesians 1:7, "In him we have redemption through his blood,
the forgiveness of sins, in accordance with the riches of
God's grace ... ' Let's reword: "Because of His blood and the
unlimited treasure, which is God's grace, our defect has been
compensated for ..." (NBV — new Bo version. HAHA!)

(3) Titus 2:14, "... who gave Himself for us to redeem us ..."

(4) 1 Tim. 2:6, "... who gave himself as a ransom for all ..."

The point: There was and is a defect. His blood, spilt on the cross,
compensated for that defect. We were lost. He purchased us back.
That is redemption!

~~~~~~~~~~~~~~~~~~~~~~~~~~~~

REFLECTION

Do you believe you need redemption?

Read Luke 15:11-32. *How does redemption play out in this story?*

renewed mind

The word "renew" is defined as:" re-start or re-establish." If we are to "re-start" and "re-establish" our mind, the question is: what is our point of reference to do so? The world says, "Think positive thoughts or ask the 'universe' for good energy." Is that our reference point? No! We, as believers, need to look no further than the cross. It is where we lay down our burdens and pick up grace. It is our re-start. It is our re-establishment of relationship and identity. Moreover, this is not a one-time renewal but yet a daily renewal. A daily engagement of relationship. A daily re-establishing of intimacy. Will we take the time and effort to do so?

day 24

Two verses:

(1) Romans 12:2, "Do not be conformed to the pattern of this world, yet be transformed by the renewing of your mind...". There is no other way! Our renewed minds changes us but even more, it has the power to transform those around us.

(2) Ephesian 1:3-5, "Blessed be the God and Father of our Lord Jesus Christ, who has blessed us in Christ with every spiritual blessing in the heavenly places, even as he chose us in him before the foundation of the world, that we should be holy and blameless before him. In love he predestined us for adoption to himself as sons through Jesus Christ, according to the purpose of his will ...". This is our re-start, our origin! Our renewed mind means knowing we have not only been blessed (aka, having a thankful heart) but grasping the knowledge that we have been chosen. We are chosen!

REFLECTION

Read Romans 12:2 again. *What patterns of, or attachments to the world affect you the most?*

How does the renewing of your mind affect your daily life?

restoration

day 25

I think of a car being restored. Now, I have no idea about this really because I am not a "car guy." However, I know a few and what I witness is this element: The time it takes, the effort put forth, the money spent, and the joy it brings! For God, I have to believe the same process is involved. Meaning this; the time it takes to restore us (yes, our spirit is instantly cleansed by His blood, but, the restoration of our mindset takes time), the effort put forth (how great an effort did He go through to leave Heaven, become man, etc..), the money spent (the riches of heaven were and still are spent on us), and the joy it brings (I wonder how much joy he truly feels when He sees a restored soul — it has to be the biggest smile in the world!).

Two verses:

(1) Col. 1:16-20, " ... to reconcile all things unto Himself." His heart is for His people to be restored and unified to a right (new covenant) relationship with Him. It always has been and always will be.

(2) 2 Cor. 5:19, " ... God was in Christ, reconciling the world unto Himself, not counting their trespasses ..." God restoring us. Amazing!

REFLECTION

What area of your life do you need restoration in?

You are worth His time and effort. Do you believe this? Why or why not?

the word

I think of a Cody Carne's song (The Cross has the Final Word);
its lyrics read, "The cross has the final word. The savior has come
with the morning light. The cross has the final word."

What final 'word' does it have? I think back before the cross. "In
the beginning was the Word, and the Word was with God, and the
Word was God." (John 1:1). This is hard for me to fathom. Before
we had anything, before God gave Moses the law, before anything
was spoken into existence, the Word existed in the expression of
Jesus. Then, Jesus shows up on the scene, with the morning light,
if you will, "... and the word became flesh and dwelt among us ..."
(John 1:14). Jesus is not only the 'beginning word' but also the
'final word.'

Matthew 5:17 reads, "Don't misunderstand why I have come. I
did not come to abolish the law of Moses or the writings of the
prophets. No, I came to accomplish their purpose." How must
people have felt when Jesus was apparently "breaking the law"
yet looking at it from a higher purpose and truth reality. How do
we feel today?

REFLECTION

How is your daily life affected by "The Word?"

Read Psalm 119 (warning, it is long). *Underline how many times
it mentions the "word" (precepts, law, commandments, rules,
statutes, testimony, promises).*

holy spirit

day 27

I think people get weirded out by Holy Spirit because, let's be honest, some have, at times, made it weird. From speaking in tongues, to falling out in the aisle, to abusing prophecy, people are often "gun-shy." However, being "gun-shy" of such an important piece of our faith can diminish the power and influence God has in our lives and a significant part of what Jesus brought by His sacrifice on the Cross. The promise of the Father was now available so that His presence might dwell in us.

Are we filled with Holy Spirit? Yes. Is there a 2nd outpouring? Seems to be. Do I understand how all that works? No. Is there evidence of speaking in tongues? Yes. Do I understand why some "get" this gift and some do not when "filled with the Spirit?" Nope. However, what does every single person seem to "get" when filled with Holy Spirit. We receive the boldness and power to witness. And, is that not the point anyway, to have a life filled with boldness so that we are witnesses to the benefits of the cross and power of the gospel. I think so!

Two verses:

(1) Acts 1:8, "But you will receive power when Holy Spirit comes on you; and you will be my witnesses ..." Boom! There it is ... the power to be a witness of the truth and love of God.

(2) John 16:7, "But very truly I tell you, it is for your good that I am going away. Unless I go away, the Advocate will not come to you; but if I go, I will send him to you." It essentially goes like this: He dies—people panic. He raises—people rejoice. He leaves again—people panic again and go sit in a room to wait on something they are promised but have no idea what it is. Holy Spirit comes as promised—the church is born! But the best part is that the same boldness and power is still available today. Yes, today!

Did you notice that in the first two paragraphs I said, "Holy Spirit" not "the Holy Spirit?" Why, you ask? We do not say "the God" or "the Jesus Christ" so why do we say "the Holy Spirit?" What if we just said 'Holy spirit.' Would that not help personify Him (as part of the Trinity as He is) and take some of the weirdness away?

~~~~~~~~~~~~~~~~~~~~~~

REFLECTION

What comes to mind when you think of Holy Spirit?

In John 16:7 (NLT), Holy spirit is referred to as the advocate. Look up the definition for advocate. How does that help your mindset when you think of Holy spirit?

salvation

day 28

Salvation is defined as: "preservation or deliverance from harm, ruin or loss." Let's think about that in terms of our Christian faith. Christ died on the cross and rose again so we could be preserved (see Psalm 91) and that we would be delivered from the harm, ruin and loss that comes from the lie of the enemy and eternal separation from God.

Three verses:

(1) Ephesians 2:8, "For it is by grace you have been saved, through faith, it is not of yourself but a gift of God." A well known verse but do we believe it? A gift we cannot earn. It has nothing to do with us yet it is all about us. One of those unbelievable paradoxes of God and the impact of the Cross.

(2) John 3:17, "God did not send his Son into the world to condemn the world but that the world may be saved through him." Jesus came to deliver us, to save us and to restore us!

(3) Philippians 2:12, " ... work out your own salvation with fear and trembling." This verse is significant to me because it reveals that salvation is not a one-and-done phenomenon. Yes, we are filled with His Spirit and saved in a moment (how does that work? Not 100% sure. It is a miracle for sure!) but then we must work it out in order for it to grow and mature. I liken it to working out my physical body. If I want to compete, grow/ mature, perform well, or just be healthy, I have to work out (move, eat right, etc.). It is a process of life not merely or only a one-time event. Why fear and trembling? Well, I think it is because we are to be in awe of the grace and gift of salvation. It should cause us to see God and ourselves rightly. As we can do that, we see our salvation in the light of eternity which forever changes our viewpoint.

REFLECTION

What does it look like for you to "work out your salvation?"

Read Psalm 91. *How is salvation (think of the above definition) seen throughout this chapter?*

peace

Jesus said, "Peace I leave with you; my peace I give to you. Not as the world gives do I give to you. Let not your hearts be troubled, neither let them be afraid." (John 14:27)

Look around at the people you know. Actually, look in the mirror. Does your life reflect peace? Is your heart troubled, anxious, afraid? I ask myself, If Jesus says, 'peace I leave with you,' then why do I not experience it?

My "working theory" is this: our peace is tied directly to where our mind is (aka: what or whom we are looking at/focusing upon). Are we focused on the "finished work" of the cross or our own efforts, failures, achievements, status, etc.

Let's make it simpler:

>Mind focused on the world = less peace or no peace.

>Mind focused on Christ = peace.

Isaiah 26:3 states it this way, "You keep him in perfect peace whose mind is stayed on you..." The simplicity of this verse may make you uncomfortable but that does not negate the truth of it. We live in a fallen world. A world often characterized by heartache and pain. That affects us. It should. But, it does not have to steal our peace. Jesus himself says, "I have said these things to you, that in me you may have peace. In the world you will have tribulation. But take heart; I have overcome the world" (John 16:33). We will have trouble. We can have peace. It matters where our mind is 'stayed.'

REFLECTION

When you are anxious or fearful (the opposite of peace), where do you find your mind focused?

How does Christ's death and resurrection offer us peace?

passion

Passion is defined as: strong/barely controllable emotion; also life/death of Christ.

day 30

I think of the movie titled: The Passion. Why does that word capture the life and death of Christ? When I say someone is passionate, what images come to mind? Does that word make you think of Jesus Christ on the cross?

Let's look at two verses which I think capture the essence of this passion:

(1) In life, John 2:13-17, "... his disciples remembered it was written; Zeal for your house will consume me." His passion for His Father's house consumed Him. Jesus watched. Jesus waited. Jesus prayed. We can learn a lot from that!

(2) In death, Hebrews 12:2, "... for the joy set before Him, he endured the cross ..." He endured the cross ... in all its pain, in all its torture, Christ's passion for us, caused joy to emerge victoriously and death to be defeated. For the joy set before Him? Really? Joy looking at the cross ... how? This is one of my favorite verses because the depth of that one statement speaks so much of His heart and His passion.

What I say often is this: Never stop pursuing His heart because He is always pursuing yours! Simply put, His passion is YOU! It always has been ... always will be!

~~~~~~~~~~~~~~~~~~~~~~~

REFLECTION

What are you passionate about?

Have you ever associated joy with the cross? If not, after reading Hebrews 12:2, how do you explain Jesus' joy?

JUST THE BEGINNING

[Jesus and] the cross is the central point of the Christian faith. Without the death and resurrection of Jesus, we would have no faith; no point of reference. As I told a friend recently, "My faith is not dependent on if God heals a person, if He answers my prayer in a certain time frame or, if I understand every Bible story. My faith is dependent on the finished work of the cross." Paul said something similar in 1 Corinthians 2:2, "For I decided to know nothing among you except Jesus and Him crucified." Christ died to redeem you. Christ arose to restore you. And, that's just the beginning of His story for you.

Lastly, it was no mistake that the first benefit I mentioned was "access" and the last benefit was "passion". We need to know first and foremost, we have been given access to God (to the heart of the Father). Without that knowledge, we will never feel known and loved. Without feeling loved and known, you can never have passion. Friends, God is not far off. He is as close as our turned attention. One glance of our eye or one prayer from our lips and it moves His heart into action. As we turn our attention toward God, toward looking at the cross ...

Pause ...

Look again and let God show you "... great and hidden things you have yet to know" (Jeremiah 33:3).

bonus Loop 1

I have a group of friends that I work out with. We have done 5k's, 10k's, half-marathons and Spartan races. Plus, lots and lots of burpees. Anytime we workout together and do more than is planned — an extra mile or three, 50 more pushups, one extra wall sit, whatever it may be — our joke is that it is part of the 'bonus loop.' The bonus loop is rarely planned; it just happens. It is an unexpected benefit. Some of my friends may disagree with the benefit part — hahaha!

And just like the 'bonus loop' when my friends and I exercise; this is your 'bonus-loop.' Enjoy!

Eyes up ... Heart Guarded ... Mind Focused. I say these words to my children often. These words are on my back-office wall, so I see them when I walk in every morning. These words remind me what I need to do every day. They are based on Proverbs 4:23-27 (NIV). It reads, "Above all else, guard your heart, for everything you do flows from it. Keep your mouth free of perversity; keep corrupt talk far from your lips. Let your eyes look straight ahead; fix your gaze directly before you. Give careful thought to the paths for your feet and be steadfast in all your ways. Do not turn to the right or the left; keep your foot from evil."

Eyes up: 'Fix your gaze.' Where? On the cross. On the person of Jesus! Matthew 6:22-23 reminds us that if the eye is healthy, so is the whole body. Simply put, where you gaze matters!

Heart Guarded: 'Everything flows from it.' Let that sink in for a moment. Ezekiel 11:17-20 tells us that He turns our heart of stone into a heart of flesh. And we all need that!

Mind Focused: 'Give careful thought.' I think of a quote by Lao-Tzu: "Watch your thoughts; they become words. Watch your words; they become actions. Watch your actions; they become habits. Watch your habits; they become character. Watch your character; it becomes your destiny." It starts with your thoughts but affects much more than that. Keep focused!

As we try to keep our eyes up, heart guarded and mind focused; doubt can creep in. Doubt that God loves us. Doubt about our worth. Doubt that we are making progress. We all have doubts. It is normal but where that doubt takes us is paramount to our health.

As my mentor (and editor of this devo) told me years ago, "The enemy has a plan and God has a plan. You get to choose each day which one to follow." Let's look at those plans.

The enemy's plan: (Division) Create doubt. That doubt leads to distortion of the truth. This distortion leads to distraction. Being distracted causes discouragement. Discouragement can cause isolation which will lead to division of relationships. (These 5 D's come from Jon Gordon's book, The One Truth)

God's plan: (Delight) Doubt happens. That doubt leads to questions which causes you to discover truth about who God is and who you are. Discovery of identity leads to diligence in pursuit of relationships. Diligence over time creates delight.

Let's sum it up the best way possible; with Jesus' own words: "The thief comes only to steal and kill and destroy. I came that they may have life and have it abundantly." (John 10:10)

bonus Loop 2

Just in case you needed more benefits (17 to be exact), here is a 2nd 'bonus loop.' You are welcome!

Psalms 23

The Lord is my Shepherd = **That's Relationship!**

I shall not want = **That's Supply!**

He makes me lie down in green pastures = **That's Rest!**

He leads me beside still waters = **That's Refreshment!**

He restores my soul = **That's Healing!**

He leads me in paths of righteousness = **That's Guidance!**

For His name sake = **That's Purpose!**

Even though I walk through the valley of the shadow of death = **That's Testing!**

I will fear no evil = **That's Protection!**

For you are with me = **That's Faithfulness!**

Your rod and staff, they comfort me = **That's Discipline!**

You prepare a table before me in the presence of my enemies = **That's Hope!**

You anoint my head with oil = **That's Consecration!**

My cup overflows = **That's Abundance!**

Surely goodness and mercy shall follow me all the days of my life = **That's Blessing!**

And I shall dwell in the house of the Lord = **That's Security!**

Forever = **That's Eternity!**

(author/source unknown)

THOUGHT LIFE

As you read through all the benefits, did you catch yourself thinking; I do not experience these benefits. Why is that? Could it be your thought life? Craig Groeschel said it this way, "Our life is always moving in the direction of our strongest thoughts. Most of life's battles are won or lost in the mind." So, what are you thinking about? Does it create space for you to experience the benefits of the cross? Remember 1 Corinthians 1:18?

Philippians 4:8 (NIV) states, "Finally, brothers and sisters, whatever is true, whatever is noble, whatever is right, whatever is pure, whatever is lovely, whatever is admirable—if anything is excellent or praiseworthy — think about such things." Can it be said any clearer than that?

I will end this how I started it. What comes to mind when you think of the cross?

Pause ...

Pause again ...

Really, what comes to mind? This is your starting place.

And from that starting place, I pray you,

"Bless the Lord ... and forget not all his benefits ..."

(Psalms 103:2)

ABOUT THE AUTHOR

Bo Bryson, DC (aka, Dr. Bo) lives in Lincoln, NE with his better half, Jennifer. Together, they have four children: Eilam, Kale, Fallon and Isley.

Dr. Bo has been in chiropractic practice for 21 years. He has learned that when one part, whether mind, body or spirit, is 'out-of-alignment,' the whole suffers. His goal is to help you: Stop Suffering & Start Living! Dr. Bo has two other publications: (1) Regain Movement, Stability & Your Life (2004. co-authored by Corey Campbell, DC). (2) Create a Trinity Lifestyle (2013). His favorite book is 'Beautiful Outlaw' by John Eldridge.

Connect with Dr. Bo via **www.trinitychiro.com** or by scanning the QR code below.

Note: Grady W. Strop also co-authored 'Discovering Your Core Values.' You can find more information at **www.rejoiceministriesinternational.com**

notes